Amcham, Apasair, Bila
or
How, Why, When

Buku 2

Book 2 - Interrogatory Part II

Chakapan Baba Ni Ari series

Baba Malay Today series

All Rights Reserved.
No part of this publication may be reproduced, stored in a retrieval system, or transmitted, in any form or by any means electronic, mechanical, photocopying, recording or otherwise, without the prior written permission of the publishers.

Theresa Fuller asserts the moral right to be identified as the author of this work.

Bare Bear Media

ISBN 978-1-9255748-16-1 - Print
ISBN 978-1-9255748-17-8 - Ebook

Cover by Helzkat Designs

Copyright September 2022©

Sincere thanks to my husband, Paul, who supported this work in every way possible. I love you.

National Library of Australia
US Library of Congress - TXu 2-336-566

Published 9th of September 2022

Introduction - Interrogatory Part II

Language is powerful.

In writing this text, I applied the SHOW don't TELL method. I wanted the reader to be able to pick up this book and begin to learn. Much as you would pick up a game and play.

Chobak.

To try.

The only rule I wish to expound is this:

Subject + Verb + (+ Object) + Question Word

or

Question Word + Subject + Verb (+ Object)

At the end of the day, have fun.

This is Baba Malay or Chakapan Baba.

YOUR language.

Baba Malay

Baba Malay is the language of my ancestors.

A language that I discovered late in 2021 was about to go extinct with fewer than a thousand speakers in the world. I took a course in Baba Malay taught by Kenneth Chan, author of BABA MALAY FOR EVERYONE. This was my start to saving Baba Malay.

But I believed much more had to be done.

The book you hold in your hands is the result of my mad persistence to save my language. While there are books out there on Baba Malay, I found little in the way for children. As a teacher, I believe that to save a language we must start with the young. I wanted a book that parents could give to their children. One I could give to my kids.

This is my attempt.

This book, however, can be used by anyone interested in learning about Baba Malay, whatever their age.

Theresa Fuller, affectionately known in the Peranakan community as Bibek Theresa.

Sydney,
29th of May, 2022

Chobak

Chobak = To Try

Contents

Introduction	3
Baba Malay	4
Amcham - How	8
Apasair - Why	10
Chobak - Amcham/Apasair	12
Bila - When	14
Chobak - Amcham/Apasair/Bila	16
Amcham - Descriptions	18
Apasair - Sample Answers	20
Bila - Sample Times	22
Pi - Go	24
Kat - At, In, On	25
Lagik - From, Still, Yet	26
Activities & Colours	27
Clothing & Some Peranakan Clothing	28
More Examples	29
About the Author	30
More books in the Baba Malay Today Series	32

AMCHAM - How?

Dog = Anjing

How = Apa Macham or Apa Macam or Apacham or Amcham

In English, we generally say "What is this thing like?" or "Describe this thing". In Baba Malay, we use "How." E.g., How is this thing like?

Question: Lu mia anjing amcham? Or Amcham lu mia anjing?
Your dog how? Or How is your dog?

Answer: Dia bagus.
He is good.

Question: Lu mia hia amcham? Or Amcham lu mia hia?
Your big brother how? Or How is your big brother?

Answer: Dia tinggi.
He is tall.

Glossary
Anjing = Dog
Bagus = Good
Dia = He/She
Lu Mia = Your
Hia = Big brother
Tinggi = Tall

AMCHAM - How?

Big Brother = Hia

Amcham lu bikin ni kueh?
How do you make this cake?

Amcham gua pi Maxwell Road?
How do I go to Maxwell Road? (Jalan may be substituted for Road.)

Amcham lu mia hia belajair?
How does your big brother study?

Amcham lu mia hia kerja?
How does your big brother work?

> Glossary
> Bikin = Make
> Belajair = Study
> Gua = I
> Kerja = Work
> Kueh = Cake
> Lu = You   Lu Mia = Your
> Ini/ni = This
> Itu/tu = That
> Pi = Go

Chakapan Baba gua mia chakapan.

APASAIR - Why?

Family = Anak-beranak

Why = Apasair or Apasal or Kenapa

Apasair lu mia anak-beranak sini?
Why is your family here?

Apasair lu mia hia lari?
Why is your big brother running?

Apasal lu pi sana?
Why are you going there? Or Why did you go there?

Glossary

Hia = Big Brother
Lari = Run/Running (Tenses is beyond this Beginner's Book.)
Lu = You
Lu Mia = Your
Pi = Go/Going
Sini = Here
Sana = There

APASAIR - Why?

Tachi = Big Sister

Sapa ni? or Ni sapa?
Who is this?

Ni gua mia tachi.
This is my big sister.

Apasair lu mia tachi bawak kereta?
Why is your big sister driving?

Kenapa dia bikin kueh?
Why did she make a cake?

Glossary

Bawak = Bring or take
Bawak Kereta = "Take car" to mean driving or drive
Bikin = Make or making
Gua mia = My
Kereta = Car
Kueh = Cake
Makan = Eat
Ni = This
Sapa = Who

CHOBAK - AMCHAM/APASAIR

Cake = Kueh

Select the correct word

How is this done?
e.g. (**Amcham**/Apasair) ni bikin?

1. How is this cake made?
   (Amcham/Apasair) ni kueh bikin?

2. Why is your dog running?
   (Amcham/Apasair) lu mia anjing lari?

3. Why are you eating cake?
   (Amcham/Apasair) lu makan kueh?

4. How do you drive?
   (Amcham/Apasair) lu bawak kereta?

5. Why do you drive?
   (Amcham/Apasair) lu bawak kereta?

Answers: 1. Amcham. 2. Apasair. 3. Apasair. 4. Amcham. 5. Apasair.

CHOBAK - AMCHAM/APASAIR

Mother = Mak

Select the correct word

1. Why is your mother here?
   (Amcham/Apasair) lu mia Mak sini?

2. How is your mother?
   (Amcham/Apasair) lu mia Mak?

3. How do you drive?
   (Amcham/Apasair) lu bawak kereta?

4. Why do you drive?
   (Amcham/Apasair) lu bawak kereta?

5. How did you do that?
   (Amcham/Apasair) lu bikin tu?

6. Why did you do that?
   (Amcham/Apasair) lu bikin itu?

Answers: 1. Apasair. 2. Amcham. 3. Amcham. 4. Apasair. 5. Amcham. 6. Apasair.

BILA - When?

Family = Anak-beranak

Bila lu datang sini?
When did you come here?

Bila lu mia anak-beranak datang?
When did you family come?

Bila lu mia anak-beranak pi?
When did your family go?

Bila dia pi kebun?
When did she go to the garden?

Bila dia datang sana?
When did he go there?

> Glossary
> Datang = Come or Coming (Lu datang means 'You come.')
> Kebun = Garden
> Sana = There
> Pi = Go or Going, so Dia Pi = He/She goes

BILA - When?

Garden = Kebun

Bila lu mia tachi pi kebun?
When did your big sister go to the garden?

Bila gua mia hia pi Katong?
When did my big brother go to Katong?

Bila dia mia tachi datang sini?
When did her big sister come here?

Bila dia datang, gua balek.
When he came, I left. Or When he comes, I will leave.

Glossary

Balek = Leave
Datang = Come
Gua Mia = My
Hia = Big brother
Pi = Go
Tachi = Big sister

CHOBAK - AMCHAM/APASAIR/BILA

Big brother = Hia
Translate into Baba Malay

1. When is your big brother coming?
2. How is she going to Orchard Road?
3. Why is your big sister going?
4. When is your family going there?
5. Why is she here?

> Answers: 1. Bila lu mia hia datang? 2. Amcham dia pi Orchard Road? 3. Apasal lu mia tachi mo pi? 4. Bila lu mia anak-beranak pi sana? 5. Apasal dia sini?

Translate into English

1. Amcham lu mia hia?
2. Apasal lu pi kebun?
3. Apasair Tachi bawak kereta?
4. Bila gua mia hia balek?
5. Bila dia pi kebun?

> Answers: 1. How is your big brother? 2. Why do you go to the garden? 3. Why does your big sister drive? 4. When did my big brother return? 5. When did he go to the garden?

Kita mo belajair Baba Malay.

CHOBAK - AMCHAM/APASAIR/BILA

Big sister = Tachi

Select the correct word

1. When did your big sister go to Seletar?
   (Amcham/Apasair/Bila) lu mia tachi pi Seletar?

2. Why did he go to Seletar?
   (Amcham/Apasair/Apasal/Bila) dia pi Seletar?

3. How did his family go to Serangoon?
   (Amcham/Apasal/Bila) dia mia anak-beranak pi Serangoon?

4. How do you all drive?
   (Apa macham/Apasair/Bila) lu orang bawak kereta?

5. When does he drive?
   (Amcham/Apasair/Bila) dia bawak kereta?

6. Why does she make cakes?
   (Amcham/Apasair/Bila) dia bikin kueh?

Answers: 1. Bila. 2. Apasair/Apasal. 3. Amcham. 4. Apa macham.
5. Bila. 6. Apasair.

AMCHAM - Descriptions

Dog = Anjing

Amcham = How (as in description)

Question:	Lu mia anjing amcham? Or Amcham lu mia anjing? Your dog how? Or How is your dog?
Answer:	Dia gemok. He is fat.
Question:	Lu mia hia amcham? Or Amcham lu mia hia? Your big brother how? Or How is your big brother?
Answer:	Dia tak tinggi. Tak pendek. (He is of average height.) He is not tall. Not short.
More e.g.s:	Amcham lu mia tachi? How is your big sister? Or Describe your big sister. Dia mia rambot panjang. Her hair is long. Dia mia chaya mungka puteh. Her complexion is fair. Dia suka pakay sarong kebaya. She likes to wear sarong kebayas.

Belajair Chakapan Baba.

AMCHAM - Descriptions continued

Big sister = Tachi

Dia mia rumah kechik.
Her house is small.

Glossary - Additional words below have been provided for practice.

Besair = Big (Note: sometimes a big house can mean a coffin instead.)
Chaya mungka = Complexion
Gemok = Fat
Kechik = Small
Kurus = Thin
Pakay = Wear
Panjang = Long
Pendek = Short
Puteh = White or fair. (Itam = Black or dark)
Rambot = Hair
Rumah = House
Sedang-sedang = Average
Suka = Like/s
Tak = Not (Generally used with verbs and adjectives)
Tinggi = Tall, Tak Tinggi = Not Tall
Rendah = Low

APASAIR - Sample Answers

Father = Bapak

Apasair/Apasal = 'Why', generally answered with 'Pasair/Because.'

Question: **Apasair** lu mia bapak makan kueh?
Why is your father eating cake?

Answer: **Pasair** dia lapair.
Because he is hungry.

Question: **Apasair** lu masak laok embok-embok?
Why are you cooking Peranakan food?

Answer: **Pasair** gua suka makan laok embok-embok.
Because I like to eat Peranakan food.

Question: Apasal lu bawak kereta?
Why are you driving?

Answer: Pasair gua mo pi kerja.
Because I must go to work.

Question: Apasair lu belajair?
Why are you studying?

APASAIR - More Sample Answers

Cake = Kueh

Answer: Pasair gua ada exam.
Because I have an exam.

Question: Apasal lu orang pi Orchard Road?
Why did you all go to Orchard Road?

Answer: Pasair kita mo beli barang-barang.
Because we want to buy things.

Glossary

Ada = Have
Barang-barang = Things
Beli = Buy
Kueh = Cake
Laok Embok-embok = Peranakan Cuisine
Lapair = Hungry
Makan = Eat
Masak = Cook
Mo = Must/Want
Pi = Go
Suka = Like   (Note: This is a beginner's book and it is impossible to cater for every question and answer.)

BILA - Sample Times

Calendar = Calendar

Bila = When (NOTE: Tenses are beyond this Beginner's Book.)

Question: Bila lu datang?
When are you coming?

Answer: Ari Satu gua mo datang.
On Monday I will come. Or I will come on Monday.

Question: Bila Ben mia bapak mo datang sini?
When is Ben's father coming here?

Answer: Tiga ari dia mo datang.
In three days he will come.

Question: Bila Nonya mia anak pi sekolah?
When will Nonya's child go to school?

Answer: Besok, Nonya mia anak pi sekolah.
Tomorrow, Nonya's child will go to school.

Question: Bila lu orang pi cinema?
When are you all going to the cinema?

Answer: Sekarang.
Now.

Dengar Chakapan Baba.

BILA - More Sample Times

Sunday = Ari Minggu

Glossary

0 = Kosong
1 = Satu
2 = Dua
3 = Tiga
4 = Ampat
5 = Lima

6 = Anam
7 = Tuju
8 = Lapan
9 = Semilan
10 = Sepuloh
11 = Sebelair, Sebelas

Monday = Ari Satu
Tuesday = Ari Dua
Wednesday = Ari Tiga
Thursday = Ari Ampat
Friday = Ari Lima
Saturday = Ari Anam
Sunday = Ari Minggu

Ari = Day
Ari Satu = Monday
Besok = Tomorrow
Kemaren = 2 days ago
Nanti = Later
Ni Ari = Today
Sekarang = Now
Semalam = Yesterday (Note: Tiga Ari means three days but Ari Tiga means Wednesday.)

PI - Go

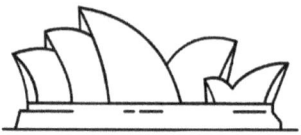

Sydney Opera House

Pi = Go (Derived from the word 'Pergi'.)
Mo Pi = Want to go

Gua pi sekolah.
I go to school.

Lu mo pi sekolah.
You want to go to school.

Lu orang tak mo pi sekolah.
You all do not want to go to school.

Gua mia anak-beranak mo pi Sydney Opera House.
My family wants to go to the Sydney Opera House.

Mana dia mia anak-beranak mo pi?
Where does her family want to go?

Glossary

Gua = I
Gua Mia = My
Mo = Want,   Tak Mo = Not Want (Tak used with verbs.)
Sekolah = School

Baba Malay is your language.

KAT - At, In, On

Family = Anak-beranak

Gua mia anak-beranak tinggair kat Joo Chiat.
My family lives at Joo Chiat.

Gua mia hia tinggair kat loteng.
My big brother lives on the floor above.

Do you live in Australia?
Lu tinggair kat Australia?

Yes, I live in Australia.
Ya, gua tinggair kat Australia.

No, I live in Singapore.
Gua tak tinggair kat Singapura.

> Glossary
> Bukan = No (Generally used with nouns and prepositions).
> Loteng = Upstairs or the floor above.
> Tinggair = Live, Tak Tinggair = Not Live
> Ya = Yes

Chakapan Baba lu mia chakapan.

LAGIK - From, Still, Yet

Kangaroo

Lagik = From (Sometimes 'Dari' can also be used.)

Gua mia tachi lagik Malaysia.
My sister is from Malaysia.

Gua beli gua mia kuching lagik keday.
I bought my cat from the shop.

I am not from Penang. I am from Singapore.
Gua bukan dari Penang. Gua lagik Singapore.

Lu datang lagik New Zealand?
Do you come from New Zealand?

Ya, gua lagik New Zealand.
Yes, I come from New Zealand.

>Glossary
>Beli = Buy
>Bukan = Not (Generally used with nouns and prepositions.)
>Datang = Come
>Keday = Shop
>Ya = Yes
>(NOTE: This book will only concentrate on 'FROM'.)

Activites

Ask = Tanya
Buy = Beli
Check = Pereksa
Close = Tutop
Cook = Masak
Come = Datang
Dance = Joget
Drink = Minom
Drive = Bawak Kereta
Eat = Makan
Enter = Masok
Gardening = Main Kebun
Knit = Kait-kait
Listen = Dengair
Open = Bukak
Play = Main
Read = Bacha
Remember = Ingat
Run = Lari
See = Nampak
Sew = Menjait
Sing = Nyanyi
Sit = Duduk
Sleep = Tidur
Study = Belajair
Swimming = Berenang
Talk = Chakap
Take Note = Sedairkan
Teach = Ajair
Think = Pikir
Try = Chobak
Work = Kerja
Write = Tulis
Understand = Reti

Colours (Orna)

The word Orna derives from the word Warna meaning colour.

Below is listed the most common words:

Black = Itam/Hitam
Blue = Biru
Brown = Chocolate
Gold = Mair/Mas
Green = Ijo
Orange = Jingga
Purple = Unggu
Red = Merah
Silver = Perak
White = Puteh
Yellow = Kuning

To get words such as pink or grey, we do the following:

Munda = Light
Tua = Dark

So pink = merah munda
i.e., a light red.

Dark gray = puteh tua

NOTE: While the word jingga describes the colour orange only and not the actual fruit, the word chocolate can be used for both the colour and the food.

Clothing

Bra = Choli
Briefs = Seluair Dalam
Brooch = Kerosang,
(Chain-linked Brooch = Kerosang Rantay)
Cap = Kopiah
Dress = Baju Dress
Earrings = Anting-anting
Glasses = Chermin Mata
Gloves = Sarong Tangan
Hat = Kopiah
Jeans = Seluair Jeans
Ring = Chinchin
Shirt = Baju +
(short-sleeved) Tangan Pendek
(long-sleeved) Tangan Panjang

Shoes = Kasot +
    (leather) Sepatu
    (Beaded) Manek
    (Slippers) Seret

Shorts = Seluair Pendek
Singlet = Baju Perap
Skirt = Skirt Panjang (Long) or
    Pendek (Short)
Socks = Buek
Sweater = Baju Sweater
Trousers = Seluair
T-Shirt = Baju T-Shirt
Umbrella = Payong
Watch = Jam Tangan

Some Peranakan Clothing

According to *A BABA MALAY DICTIONARY*, the Baju Nonya is the Baju Panjang.

Baju = Garment

Baju Kebaya = A short blouse worn with a sarong (worn by ladies).

Baju Lok Chuan = Loose Chinese jacket and trousers of silk worn by Babas on festive occasions.

Baju Panjang = 3/4 length Nonya dress worn with a sarong.

Sarong = Long piece of cloth wrapped around the body generally tucked around the waist or under the armpits.
See image below.

More Examples

Gua mia hia suka pakay baju Lok Chuan.
My big brother likes to wear the Lok Chuan.

Chantek sair gua mia tachi pakay kebaya.
My big sister looks beautiful wearing the kebaya.

Dia pakay anting-anting perak.
She wears silver earrings.

Dia tak suka pakay sarong tangan bila dia main kebun.
He does not like to wear gloves when he gardens.

Bila gua mia anak-beranak pi Australia, kita semua pakay baju sweater.
When my family went to Australia, we all wore sweaters.

Lu mo pakay kasot manek sama baju kebaya?
Do you want to wear beaded shoes with the baju kebaya?

Lu bolih bacha buku jingga tu?
Can you read that orange book?

Jorang semua pakay chermin mata.
They all wear glasses.

> Glossary
> Chantek = Beautiful
> Pakay = Wear
> Sair = A term used for emphasis
> Sama = With
> Semua = All
> Suka = Like/s

Forms of Questions in English

In English there are many ways of asking questions. Unfortunately, not all these question words have their Baba Malay equivalent.

Are = No Baba Malay equivalent
Can = Boleh
Could = Boleh
Do = No Baba Malay equivalent
Did = No Baba Malay equivalent
Have = Ada
How = Apa Macham or Amcham
Is = No Baba Malay equivalent
Was = No Baba Malay equivalent
Were = No Baba Malay equivalent
What = Apa
When = Bila
Where = Mana
Why = Apasair or apasal
Will = Boleh

    Examples:

Are you coming?
Lu mo datang?

Can you come?
Boleh lu datang?

Could you come?
Boleh lu datang?

Do you want to come?
Lu mo datang?

    (Note: Lu = You, Lu Datang = You come, Mo = Want)

About the Author

Theresa Fuller

Theresa Fuller has always loved stories and story-telling, but it was not until the birth of her first son that she became a full-time writer. Her aim was to write stories about her culture: Southeast Asia.

Theresa was Head of Computing at various private schools in Sydney. She has also been a Higher School Certificate (HSC) Examiner and HSC Assessor. Her teaching degrees have seen her work in primary and secondary schools and at Kalgoorlie College in Western Australia.

Her first published novel in 2018 was *THE GHOST ENGINE*, a steampunk fantasy about the fictitious granddaughter of Ada Lovelace, the world's first programmer. Theresa has published books on Southeast Asian mythology: *THE GIRL WHO BECAME A GODDESS* (2019), *THE GIRL SUDAN PAINTED LIKE A GOLD RING* (2022) and *EATING THE LIVER OF THE EARTH* - collection of the lost folktales of the mousedeer Sang Kanchel.

In 2023, *WHERE CRANES WEAVE AND BAMBOO SINGS* a visual narrative textbook for children and beginner writers was published.

In 2020, Theresa lost many family members. She threw heself into researching her family history as a way to deal with her grief. This was when she discovered that the language of her ancestors - Baba Malay - was on the verge of extinction. As a writer, teacher and selfpublishing author, Theresa found herself in an unusual position - she was able to create the curriculum that was needed to help fill a vacuum.

The result is the **Baba Malay Today** series. And now the **New Peranakan Tales** series starting with GUA PI KEDAY.

All in aid of saving the language.

www.theresafuller.com

Thank you for your support!

More Books in the Baba Malay Today Series

Book 1 - Interrogatory Part I   SAPA, APA, MANA or
WHO, WHAT, WHERE

Book 2 - Interrogatory Part II   AMCHAM, APASAIR, BILA or
HOW, WHY, WHEN

Book 3 - Conjunctions   TAPI, ABIS, PASAIR or
BUT, SO, BECAUSE

Book 4 - Prepositions   ATAIR, KAT, BAWAH or
TOP, NEAR, BOTTOM

Book 5 - Antonyms   ALUS, KA, KASAR or
DELICATE, OR, COARSE

Book 6 - Essence   CHAKAPAN BABA ATI or
THE HEART OF BABA MALAY

Book 7 - Poetry   CHAKAPAN BABA PANTON or
BABA MALAY POETRY

Book 8 - Idioms   CHAKAPAN BABA CHAKAPAN or
BABA MALAY IDIOMS

Dear Reader,

Thank you for the purchase of this book.

Please help us spread the word as we try to save our language.

Bibek Theresa

Sydney, 18th of June, 2022

Jangan lupa Chakapan Baba.

www.ingramcontent.com/pod-product-compliance
Lightning Source LLC
Chambersburg PA
CBHW070341120526
44590CB00017B/2981